Christmas in the 1930's

Written by Aron Froese   Illustrated by Jessie Froese

Written by Aron Froese
Book Cover by Jessie Froese
Illustrations by Jessie Froese
Forward by Gary Froese
Photographs provided by Marlene Froese

ISBN 979-8-9923586-0-5

Printed via IngramSpark

1st edition 2025

This book is made for

Mary Froese in honored memory of her beloved husband
Aron (1931-2015)

Thank you for creating such a loving family to be part of.
We love you immensely.

Foreword

By Gary Froese

This illustrated recreation of an old favourite Christmas poem was completed by my father Aron Froese back in the 1960's. My dad loved poetry and stories from his youth growing up in the Canadian prairies. As his kids and grandkids, we would hear portions of stories from him during family visits. He took this well-known poem and personalized it from the experiences of his many Christmases growing up in the 1930s. Thank you to our daughter-in-law Jessie for completing this labour of love by illustrating this great poem.

Aron Peter Froese and Katerina Froese (Aron's father and mother

The immediate family (Aron second on right

Aron and his twin brother Ben

It was the day before Christmas
When out west in the woods,
My father came home,
The sleigh laden with goods.

The horses all frosted
From head to toe,
The sleigh runners crunched
As they slid over the snow.

The sun was just setting
Itself in the west.
The birds in the treetops
Had settled to rest.

The lights for this traveler
Were the stars in the sky.
The farm dogs they barked
To all passersby.

The lakes they were frozen,
And nature seemed dead.
The cattle at home
In the barn had been fed.

Money was scarce in those days
Of nineteen thirty.
The seed grain had been cleaned,
But the crops turned out dirty.

The rains had not come
For the crops to mature.
And winters seemed long
For a family to endure.

My father was whistling
A tune of the season,
For deep down inside,
He did have a good reason.

For hands that were strong,
And a mind that was bright.
He had whittled out toys,
In the cold winter nights.

The children all well,
And a wife who could cook.
This you can be sure,
She hadn't learned from a book.

The baking was done
For this big event.
We all had been taught
Why the Christ child was sent.

The hope He had brought us,
In this age today,
Can never be measured,
In a mathematical way.

The End

Above: Part of the family in front of their home

Bottom left: Aron and wife Mary

Bottom Right: Aron in his early 20's

www.ingramcontent.com/pod-product-compliance
Lightning Source LLC
Chambersburg PA
CBHW041613120626
46551CB00002B/435